WITHDRAWN

Gloria Steinem

Gloria Steinem

FEMINIST EXTRAORDINAIRE

by Caroline Lazo

Lerner Publications Company • Minneapolis

TO ELLY

The author and publisher would like to give special thanks to Gloria Steinem for her help and kindness in assisting with this project.

Website address: www.lernerbooks.com

Library of Congress Cataloging-in-Publication Data

Lazo, Caroline Evensen.
    Gloria Steinem / Caroline Lazo.
      p.   cm.
    Includes bibliographical references and index.
    Summary: Recounts the life of the feminist leader, her impact on
the women's movement, and the founding of *Ms.* magazine and the Ms.
Foundation.
      ISBN 0-8225-4934-4
      1. Steinem, Gloria—Juvenile literature. 2. Feminists—United
States—Biography—Juvenile literature.   [1. Steinem, Gloria.
2. Feminists. 3. Women—Biography.] I. Title.
HQ1413.S675L39 1998
305.42'092—dc21
[B]   97–16831

Manufactured in the United States of America
1 2 3 4 5 6 – JR – 03 02 01 00 99 98

CONTENTS

Steinem, left, celebrates the 10th anniversary of Ms. *magazine with cofounder Patricia Carbine, right. Actress Loretta Swit is in the center.*

"THE STAGE IS SET"

ON JUNE 4, 1982, 1200 PEOPLE GATHERED AT THE Armory on historic Park Avenue in New York City to celebrate the 10th anniversary of *Ms.* magazine—and to honor Gloria Steinem, Patricia Carbine, and its other pioneering cofounders. *Ms.,* the first national magazine published and edited entirely by women since Susan B. Anthony's *The Revolution,* had taken giant steps in the promotion of the right of women and girls to equal treatment and full humanity. It had become a far-reaching voice for the women's movement in the United States.

Steinem's writings and those of other feminists did more than call attention to women's issues. They called for action, and they called for change. "Now," she reminded *Ms.* readers, "there are women astronauts . . . women police officers . . . women doctors . . . and for the first time in our history a woman is a justice of the United States Supreme Court." Ten years earlier, such feats had

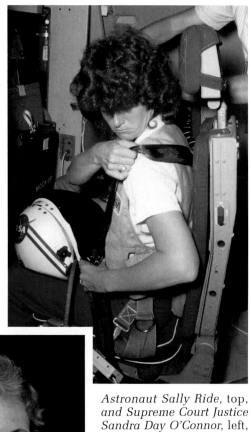

Astronaut Sally Ride, top, and Supreme Court Justice Sandra Day O'Connor, left, represent the progress women have made in entering fields of employment that had formerly been open only to men.

existed only in one's dreams. "Now," she proclaimed, "we have a past to celebrate—and a big future to plan. It's the end of the beginning. The stage is set."

The *Ms.* anniversary marked a milestone in Steinem's life—a personal achievement that would have been impossible to foresee during her difficult childhood in Ohio. While caring for her mentally ill mother in an old house plagued by rats, a leaky roof, and a faulty furnace, Steinem had had little time to think about the future. But she always knew that her parents valued and loved her. As she noted later, "With enough sun and water to put down deep roots of self-esteem, children can withstand terrible storms."

Steinem's father, Leo, had brought the sun into her life, if only sporadically. He liked fun and adventure, and had treated his younger daughter like a pal. Leo loved show business, and as the owner of a summer resort at Clarklake, Michigan, he had contact with a variety of performers and popular bands. When Gloria Steinem was born, her parents announced the event in true, theatrical style: "Gloria Marie Steinem . . . March 25, 1934 . . . World Premier Appearance . . ."

And the curtain rose.

Gloria's parents, Ruth and Leo Steinem, shortly after their 1921 marriage

FAMILY TIES

STEINEM'S PARENTS FIRST MET AT THE UNIVERSITY of Toledo in Ohio in 1917. Leo was the editor of the college newspaper, and Ruth Nuneviller became its literary editor. But it was her spirit of adventure and creative mind that attracted the fun-loving Leo Steinem.

Because Leo came from a wealthy Jewish family and Ruth came from a working-class Christian one, their 1921 marriage was criticized by many—including members of both their families. In the 1920s, people in most American communities frowned upon "mixed marriages."

After graduation, Ruth taught college math for a year to satisfy an agreement she had made with her mother. But Ruth did not enjoy teaching, so she became a reporter and wrote for the *Toledo Blade.* She loved being a journalist, but she took a year off when her first child, Susanne, was born in 1925. That same year Leo Steinem bought land at Clarklake, Michigan, an isolated rural area about 50 miles from Toledo. He wanted to develop a summer resort there that would attract big-name bands and give people for miles around a place to dance to what was then the nation's most popular music.

Leo built Ocean Beach Pier in 1928, but his timing was not good. The stock market crashed in 1929, and the Great Depression of the 1930s began. Ruth worried about their financial situation. She tried to fulfill three full-time roles as wife, mother, and newspaper reporter, but this was impossible and the strain proved too great.

In 1930, Leo and Ruth sold their Toledo house and moved to Clarklake, because it cost less to live there. Soon after the move, Ruth gave birth to a stillborn son. The tragedy had lasting effects. Ruth became unable to sleep, and she dreaded being left alone. She had her first nervous breakdown that same year, when Susanne was five. Ruth spent many months in a Toledo sanitarium before returning to Clarklake.

Gloria's "world premier" arrival in 1934 delighted friends and family alike—especially her nine-year-old sister, Susanne. Susanne had begged for a baby sister for years, and finally her wish had come true. Although her parents wanted to name the new baby Cynthia, they let Susanne name her Gloria, after a favorite doll. "Gloria was certainly a beautiful, cheerful baby, seen in early pictures reaching out eagerly toward chickens, sheep, dogs, horses," wrote biographer Carolyn Heilbrun. Early pictures of the sisters show a warm, close relationship, in spite of their age difference.

Leo Steinem built Ocean Beach Pier in 1928. Although the resort eventually failed, Gloria spent several happy summers there.

Spending summers at the family's resort at Clarklake was like "running wild," Steinem said, recalling her childhood there. She often wandered into the dance hall, where musicians rehearsed for shows at the resort. Steinem also mastered tap-dance steps taught to her by Ruby Brown, who sold cigarettes and cigars. She also played on the beach and spent whole days in her bathing suit. She loved the freedom to explore the beaches and to play as she pleased. Even in her childhood, Steinem had a sense of independence and took responsibility for herself.

The warm summers at the lake contrasted sharply with the harsh, cold winters there. In winter, the Steinems headed for California or Florida in a house trailer. Leo

Ruth and Gloria poke their heads out of the family trailer, which the family lived and traveled in during the winter.

made a living by buying and selling antiques as they drove across the country, but that lifestyle was not easy on Ruth. She longed for financial security and a normal home environment, and she suffered from depression and anxiety. Life on the road kept Gloria and Susanne out of school for long periods of time, but Ruth had a teaching certificate so she taught her daughters their lessons. She also taught them to love books and learning.

Susanne left home to attend Smith College in Northampton, Massachusetts, when Gloria was eight.

Ruth knew that Smith was one of the best women's colleges in the country, and Susanne's acceptance there thrilled her. Still, Ruth hated to see Susanne leave home.

Gloria missed having friends and sharing school activities, but she loved following her father around as he made his sales and planned his travels. He was fun—full of comic routines and creative ideas—but he was unable to turn his ideas into permanent income. Finally, World War II and gas rationing put an end to Leo's resort. Many men joined the armed forces and fought overseas, and

The Steinem family shortly before Susanne left for Smith College. From left to right, *Ruth, Leo, Susanne, and Gloria*

women took men's places on assembly lines. Because troops needed fuel to fight the war, there was a gas shortage in the United States. As a result, people could not get gas for long drives to vacation resorts. After Leo's resort closed, holding the family together caused more stress than he or Ruth could handle. In 1944 they separated. Ruth and Gloria moved from Clarklake to a small house in Amherst, Massachusetts, to be near Susanne, who was a junior at Smith in nearby Northampton. When Susanne found a summer job in New York City, Ruth moved Gloria to a house in Scarsdale, New York, that belonged to an old college classmate who was away for the summer.

Gloria felt sad about her parents' separation, but they had aways seemed too different to be together. Even at the age of 10, she seemed prepared to take on more responsibilities in her father's absence. In her essay, "Ruth's Song (Because She Could Not Sing It)," Steinem recalled those trying times:

> My father had patiently brought home the groceries and kept our odd household going until I was eight or so and my sister went away to college. Two years later when wartime gas rationing closed his summer resort and he had to travel to buy and sell in summer as well as winter, he said: "How can I travel and take care of your mother? How can I make a living?" He was right. It was impossible to do both. I did not blame him for leaving once I was old enough to be the bringer of meals. . . .

Leo took this photo of Gloria in front of their Clarklake house

Even as a young girl, Steinem seemed to sense the power of love as a healer of differences: "He treated me like a grown-up," she wrote about her father, "and I loved him for it. . . . Even in the hardest times . . . I knew with a child's unerring sense of fairness that he was treating me as well as he treated himself. . . . Against all convention for raising children, and especially little girls, he loved and honored me as a unique person. And that let me know that he and I—and men and women—are not opposites at all."

Ruth was plagued by fear and depression. She often heard imaginary voices. At other times, she didn't sleep for days because of her fears. Frightening images almost never left her mind, and while they may not have caused Ruth's depression, Gloria was certain they made it worse.

Modern medications for anxiety, depression, and other mental illnesses were not available in the 1940s, so Ruth relied on the treatment at hand—mainly, on "Doc Howard's medicine." The medicine helped her sleep, but it also made her appear drunk when she was awake, causing embarrassing moments when Gloria's friends were around.

Ruth's House

In the fall of 1945, Gloria and Ruth moved into a basement apartment in Toledo, Ohio, close to Monroe School, where Gloria attended sixth grade. Ruth and Gloria slept in a bunk bed, because the "apartment" was in fact a small room behind the furnace. Little space remained for anything else. Gloria once pretended to be sick because she fantasized that her mother might suddenly become healthy and bring her chicken soup. But that didn't happen. "I knew that my mother loved me, but that she couldn't take care of me," Steinem later commented.

Like her dad, Gloria always expected better days ahead. The following year, when she and her mother moved from the basement apartment into the family house that Ruth had inherited, Gloria believed life was bound to be happier. She also believed that her mother was bound to get better.

The house was old, rundown, and badly in need of repairs, but Ruth had inherited it, so it was hers to keep. In spite of its shabby condition—including a dangerous furnace that often failed to work in winter—Ruth was able to rent two small apartments carved out of the first floor of the house. She and Gloria lived on the second floor. The monthly income from tenants provided money for Gloria and her mother during the seven years they lived together in Toledo. Ruth and Leo had divided the property in Michigan, so there was also a small income from the people who had leased land to build summer cottages.

Gloria attended Monroe School and finally had time to see friends. But books were still her best companions. They allowed her to escape—if only momentarily—from her heavy responsibilities at home. Her mother's spells of anxiety, depression, and agoraphobia (fear of leaving home) grew worse, but Gloria tried her best to take care of Ruth and study at the same time. Steinem later wrote:

Gloria playing the piano in Amherst, Massachusetts, in 1945

I remember a long Thanksgiving weekend spent hanging on to her with one hand and holding my eighth-grade assignment of *A Tale of Two Cities* in the other, because the war outside our house was so real to my mother that she had plunged her hand through a window, badly cutting her arm in an effort to help us escape. Only when she finally agreed to take her medicine could she sleep, and only then could I end the terrible calm that comes with crisis and admit to myself how afraid I had been.

Living alone with Ruth (from 1944 to 1951) was not easy for Gloria, but she made the most of every moment. She haunted the local library and read the novels of Louisa May Alcott—especially *Little Women,* which she had read many times before. Gloria identified with Jo's longing for independence, and her spirit of adventure. But above all, Gloria loved "the sisterly chats," as Alcott called them, that brought that book to life. And in almost every work by the nineteenth-century British writer Charles Dickens, Gloria found some aspect of poverty similar to her own.

But it was through her tap dancing, begun at the Clark-lake resort, that Gloria found special joy—and some income, too. Her charming smile and natural grace endeared her to audiences of all ages, and she danced at community events as well as school programs at Waite High School in Toledo. She also performed with her dance class at the local Eagles Club, and she paid for her dance lessons with the $10 per show she earned there. In

Heilbrun's book *The Education of a Woman,* Steinem
remembered those nights:

> We danced while the band [was] . . . out drinking; we
> did our little show in front of the circular bandstand.
> From the floor to the ceiling the bandstand was cov-
> ered with chicken wire; otherwise, when the guys out
> front had a fight, and they always did, someone
> would be thrown through the bass drum. We danced
> in front of the chicken wire; we were earlier in the
> evening, it didn't get bad until midnight.

Even Ruth—"in a good period"—got into the act. She
assisted her daughter when Gloria starred in some bibli-
cal plays—"doing several corny performances of *Noah's
Ark* while my proud mother shook metal sheets backstage
to make thunder."

Performing with other dance students gave Gloria a certain sense of self-confidence. Already five feet seven
inches tall in her early teens, she was able to pass for 18
and dance in the chorus of summertime operettas. At 16,
she was even able to enter a beauty pageant. She entered
the pageant hoping that she would win a way out of
Toledo and to the next stage of the contest. Although she
was aware that people thought she was attractive, Gloria
never thought her appearance was as important as other
traits. She felt she also needed to dance and to study hard
in school. Just the chance to get away from her dreary
home environment—even for a few hours—was a wel-
come change.

Gloria, right, poses with friends at a Michigan Girl Scout camp in 1946. Camp provided a much-needed break from her life in Toledo.

Winters in the Toledo house were almost unbearable. When rats found their way into the halls, Gloria tried to barricade the end of her bed to keep them from biting her feet. (She had been bitten once, and that experience had

terrified her.) Her mother's battle with anxiety and irra-
tional thoughts grew worse. There were times, Gloria
recalled, when Ruth

> woke in the early dark, too frightened and disori-
> ented to remember that I was at my usual after-school
> job, and so called the police to find me. Humiliated
> in front of my friends by sirens and policemen, I
> would yell at her—and she would bow her head in
> fear and say "I'm sorry, I'm sorry, I'm sorry," just as
> she had done so often when my otherwise-kind-
> hearted father had yelled at her in frustration. Per-
> haps the worst thing about suffering is that it finally
> hardens the hearts of those around it.

At the end of her junior year at Waite High School,
Gloria was juggling more homework, part-time jobs, and
the growing responsibility for her mother's care. Then the
church next door bought the old house in which they
lived. The church planned to tear it down, and they had
to move. Her sister, Susanne, then "performed a miracle."
Susanne asked Leo to come to Toledo and take Ruth to
California for one year—giving Gloria a chance to stay
with her sister in Washington, D. C., and finish her senior
year in high school there. Susanne had a tough time con-
vincing Leo, because he had removed himself completely
from their lives and was barely able to cope on his own.
Yet out of deep, abiding love for his daughter, he said yes.
He knew that Gloria, who had never asked for any favors,
deserved one now.

Ruth sold the family house in Toledo—with the understanding that the money would be applied to Gloria's future education. Leo arranged to take Ruth to California for a year. Although the situation called for taking on more responsibility than he wanted to handle, he did not let his daughters down. "But one year is all," he told Gloria. "We're synchronizing our watches."

To Gloria, one year away from her East Toledo neighborhood was more than she ever dreamed of—a miracle indeed. But certain questions began to haunt her. Would she like her new school? Would she fit in with the other students already entrenched in their senior year? Would she have to explain her odd family situation? Would the money hold out?

Gloria's high school graduation picture. She graduated from Western High School in Washington, D.C., in 1952.

CHAPTER TWO

AWAY FROM HOME

"... for to be independent and earn the praise of those she loved were the deepest wishes of her heart, and this seemed to be the first step toward that happy end."

—Louisa May Alcott, *Little Women*

FOR GLORIA, ARRIVING IN WASHINGTON WAS LIKE landing on another planet, light-years away from Toledo, Ohio. Through Susanne and her friends, Gloria discovered a whole new life—full of parties, laughter, and new friends. When she entered Western High School in 1951, the students and teachers immediately liked her. When she was elected vice president of her senior class, no one was happier—or more surprised—than Gloria.

The summer following her graduation from high
school, Gloria immersed herself in the 1952 Democratic
presidential campaign of Adlai Stevenson, former governor of Illinois. Like many other thoughtful young people,
she admired his brilliant mind and sense of fairness. But
his opponent was General Dwight D. Eisenhower, a popular World War II hero who was not used to losing battles.

Undaunted, Gloria worked hard while energizing
others. She began to learn how to capture the attention
of voters, use her writing skills in a newsletter called
"Students for Stevenson," and counteract an opponent's

*After her high school graduation, Gloria became involved in the cam-
paign of Democratic presidential candidate Adlai Stevenson.*

distortions without losing her cool—lessons she continued to use in later years. The campaign newsletter informed students about Stevenson's stand on issues and aroused their interest in national affairs.

Working for the campaign kept Gloria's mind off her biggest worry—college. She hoped to go to Smith, Susanne's alma mater. Gloria was afraid her unspectacular grades at Western High School, her college entrance exam scores, and the fact that Waite High School had never before placed a student at Smith would keep her out, but she was accepted. In the fall of 1952, she entered Smith College—a feat that thrilled the whole family—especially Ruth.

As Gloria's last year in high school ended, Ruth's year in Leo's care came to an end. Ruth moved in with Gloria and Susanne for the summer. Later, Susanne researched and found a hospital in nearby Baltimore, Maryland, where Ruth was treated for an anxiety disorder. As Ruth improved over the next two years, she was able to attend social events in Washington, D.C., and to enjoy visits with Gloria, Susanne and her husband, Bob Patch, and the first of their six children. Eventually, Susanne and Bob built a separate apartment for Ruth in their new house. Knowing that Ruth was well cared for gave Gloria a great sense of relief.

With increased self-confidence after her year in Washington, Gloria welcomed college life with an open mind, and she made new friends easily. But a few of her friends, like many "Smithies" at the time, had been raised in wealthy households with servants and doting parents. When conversations focused on home life, Gloria decided to put a humorous spin on hers—the way her father might have done. Soon her "tales of Toledo" became a great source of interest and amusement.

To her surprise, Gloria discovered that certain parts of her past—even hanging out backstage at the Clarklake resort shows—served her well at Smith. In a 1964 article for *Glamour* magazine, "College and What I Learned There," she recalled:

> Once there, I discovered that my experience could be put to use because it did not duplicate the experiences of others. My French, for instance, which I had learned in a classful of Korean veterans returning to high school on the G.I. Bill . . . was not good. I made an arrangement with a freshman who had been raised by an English nanny and tutored by a mademoiselle. She helped me with my French grammar and translations. In return, I made her up each time she went out with her New York fiancé (a little training in stage makeup can work wonders) . . . and taught her how to iron, a skill with which she was so delighted that she ironed my dresses, too. This cheerful bargain was the beginning of an important lesson: Don't worry about your background; whether it's odd or ordinary, use it, build on it.

At Smith, Gloria developed a strong interest in international relations. Although her work for Adlai Stevenson's

Gloria Steinem's graduation photo as it appeared in the Smith College yearbook. She majored in government.

campaign ended with Eisenhower's election in November 1952, the seeds of her later involvement with politics had been planted.

Gloria's curiosity about people from different cultures—their customs and ideas—was profound. During her junior year, she had the opportunity to spend a year in Switzerland with more than a dozen other Smith students. By that time, she had raised her grades to A's and B's. But again, worry about money plagued her, and she applied for scholarships to cover the cost of her senior year. In the meantime, she enjoyed living with a French family in Paris before going on to the University of

Steinem, left, on graduation day at Smith, June 3, 1956. She is shown here with a classmate.

Geneva in Switzerland. Her favorite course at the university was international law. When the courses ended, she earned a scholarship at Oxford University for a summer course on the literature and politics of twentieth-century England. She spent the summer studying there before returning to Smith in the fall of 1955.

Much to her relief, Gloria received funding for her senior year. That same year, she met Blair Chotzinoff. They met on a blind date arranged by Smith classmate Nancy Gary. Blair's quick wit, fun-loving spirit, and nurturing and considerate nature attracted Gloria immediately. They later became engaged.

Gloria had dated other men while in college, but Blair ranked high above the rest—and he proved it with great style. As a pilot with the Air National Guard, he flew on weekends. On one of those flights, he wrote "Gloria" in the sky above the Smith campus.

Gloria's life seemed to fit the pattern of most 1950s college women who planned to get married soon after graduation. Some women even quit school to marry before graduation. Gloria, however, could never understand why anyone would leave college, where the promise of three meals a day was always fulfilled and all the best books were available day and night.

High academic achievement marked Gloria's senior year. She was elected to the honor society Phi Beta Kappa and graduated *magna cum laude*, "with great distinction." Her political science major set her apart from most college women, who, in the 1950s, considered government courses to be the province of men. Her outlook placed her ahead of her time. On graduation day, June 3, 1956, she felt pride in what she had accomplished and excitement about the years ahead. Her mother, father, and sister were there to share the special moment, and they applauded loudly as Gloria accepted her degree.

Years later, in *Revolution from Within,* Gloria recalled graduation day at Smith:

> On the New England campus of Smith College, I realized again the great distance between this idyllic scene and my old neighborhood. Green lawns, landmark buildings, new graduates carrying long-stemmed roses, and smiling alumnae in summer dresses—all seemed evidence of assurance and good fortune. But underneath, there were doubts and tensions. And underneath was where we had been trained to keep them.

As plans for her marriage to Blair began to take shape, Gloria backed out. She had fallen deeply in love, but she suddenly realized the magnitude of a marriage commitment. There was still so much of the world she wanted to see and study. Unlike her classmates, she did not warm to the idea of motherhood. Gloria had already been a mother—to her own mother—with all the responsibilities that had entailed. Gloria thought it would be unfair to both Blair and herself to marry without being ready to accept that commitment. Since she didn't feel ready, she broke off the engagement the summer after graduation, but their strong feeling for each other remained.

Later that summer, Gloria won a special one-year fellowship to study in India the following year. In the fall of 1956, she left for that country—a journey that she later said "opened up the world to me."

In Gandhi's Footsteps

While waiting for her visa to travel through India, Steinem visited friends in London. Soon after her arrival, however, she discovered that she was pregnant. She felt desperate, but she knew she could not give up all her plans, return to the United States, and marry Blair. She knew that she was not ready for marriage and motherhood. She also knew that in the 1950s, having a child out of wedlock was shameful and would put her in the same position as her mother: poor and alone with a child.

Abortion was illegal in the United States, but in England the procedure was allowed by obtaining permission in writing from two doctors. After carefully studying this option, she found a compassionate doctor who asked only that she keep it a secret. The abortion experience was the first time Gloria felt she had really taken responsibility for her own life. Then, her only wish was to continue her travels and learn more about India.

Steinem admired Mohandas Gandhi, one of the great political and spiritual leaders of the twentieth century.

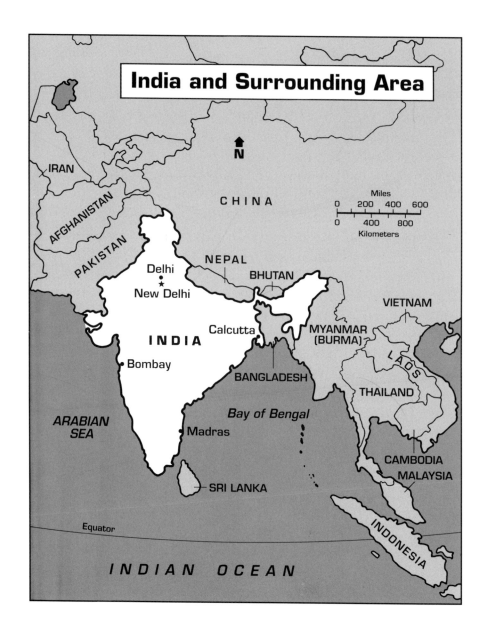

India and Surrounding Area

N

IRAN

CHINA

Miles
0   200   400   600
0   400   800
Kilometers

AFGHANISTAN

PAKISTAN

Delhi
New Delhi

NEPAL

BHUTAN

VIETNAM

INDIA

Calcutta

MYANMAR
(BURMA)

LAOS

Bombay

BANGLADESH

THAILAND

ARABIAN
SEA

Bay of Bengal

Madras

CAMBODIA
MALAYSIA

SRI LANKA

INDONESIA

Equator

INDIAN OCEAN

On February 4, 1957, Gloria arrived in Bombay, the largest city in India. From there she flew to New Delhi, the capital city, where she began her studies at the University of Delhi with Kayla Achter, who was a co-fellowship student from Smith. When Steinem's courses ended three months later, she traveled for a short time with Kayla. Eventually Gloria decided to explore India on her own to learn about the people—particularly the followers of Mohandas Gandhi.

Mohandas Gandhi was one of the most important spiritual and political leaders of the twentieth century—and one whom Steinem admired greatly. Gandhi helped free India from British control by a unique method of nonviolent disobedience. This method included nonpayment of taxes, refusing to go to British schools and courts, and defying British rule by organizing nonviolent sit-ins in the streets. The independence movement began on a small scale, but Gandhi changed it into a mass movement of millions of Indians. Gandhi led by example, and his commitment to the equal rights of all Indians endeared him to the people. The whole world mourned his death by an assassin's bullet in January 1948. Gandhi's ability to put his beliefs into action for the good of all Indians had impressed Steinem, and in India she had the opportunity to see the results of his work and meet the people who had been his disciples.

Steinem spent about a month in the city of Calcutta, then traveled south by train to Madras. Many Indians had told her that this area was the "real India." Eventually

Steinem wore a sari and sandals, the traditional dress of Indian women, during most of her stay in India.

Steinem arrived at Gandhigram, where she met a group of Gandhi's followers. The people she met welcomed her warmly. Gloria decided to wear a sari and sandals, the traditional dress of Indian women, throughout most of her stay in India. Living and talking with Gandhi's followers gave Steinem a chance to see how his principle of *Satyagraha,* or "soul force," had inspired them to win independence from Britain. She also learned how the Indian people were still using Gandhi's principle of nonviolent resistance to protest unfair laws on a local level.

Led by Vinoba Bhave, a Gandhi disciple, a group of Indians from many different religions walked from village to village, listening to the people and encouraging their pursuit of equal rights and freedom from fear. "The question was," Steinem reflected in *Moving beyond Words,* "Would I go with them? Bhave's coworkers assured me I wouldn't seem any more odd than others from outside the area. . . . Besides, part of their mission was to show villagers that people outside this isolated area [Ramnad, in southern India] knew and cared what was happening to them."

Steinem joined the group, and the experience, she later reported, had an unforgettable impact on her life:

> Each day, we set off along paths shaded by palms and sheltered by banyan trees, cut across plowed fields, and waded into streams to cool off and let our homespun clothes dry on us as we walked. In the villages, families shared their food and sleeping mats with us, women taught me how to wash my sari and wash and oil my hair, and shopkeepers offered us rice cakes and sweet, milky tea in the morning. I found there was a freedom in having no possessions but a sari, a cup, and a comb, and even in the midst of turmoil, a peacefulness in focusing only on the moment at hand. I remember this as the first time in my life when I was living completely in the present.

For the first time in years, Steinem's haunting worry about money vanished—at least temporarily. She focused on her Indian friends and their questions and concerns. They often asked questions about American society and how it was structured. Were people from all cultural backgrounds treated equally? Was America really "the land of the free?" Such questions made Steinem think about her country from a whole new perspective:

> Because India had accustomed me to seeing a rainbow of skin colors, I was also realizing belatedly that in my own multiracial country, you could go snowblind from white faces in any business area or "good" neighborhood. . . . Indians described nuances of color as unselfconsciously as any other aspect of appearance.

Before leaving India, Steinem wrote *The Thousand Indias,* a travel guide published by the Indian government and designed to attract Americans to study and travel in India, as she had. The book was an introduction to the great variety of people, customs, and ideas found in India. In writing the book, Steinem discovered her talent to persuade people through the written word. Because of her impressive writing ability, she was able to get more writing assignments and other part-time jobs, which made it possible for her to stay in India one more year. When Steinem finally left India, she carried these wise Gandhian messages with her—indelible in her mind:

- If you want people to listen to you, you have to listen to them.
- If you hope people will change how they live, you have to know how they live.
- If you want people to see you, you have to sit down with them eye-to-eye.

Steinem's travels in India formed a major turning point in her life. "Most of us," she wrote, "have a few events that divide our lives into 'before' and 'after.' This was one for me."

Exploring New York

In 1958 Steinem returned to the United States. She stopped in Washington to see her family and then moved to New York, where she slept on the floor in friends' apartments. She hoped to work to improve the lives of others, as she had done in India. She also hoped to use her writing skills. But as Carolyn Heilbrun noted, "In the fifties, women weren't hired for 'important' jobs, and college graduates appeared overqualified for the 'unimportant'. . . ones." Serious topics were covered by male journalists—not "girl reporters"—as Steinem discovered when looking for freelance writing assignments.

Disappointed by the lack of job offers and "too broke and impatient" to stay in New York, Steinem accepted a job in Cambridge, Massachusetts, offered to her by members of the National Student Association (NSA). They had formed the Independent Research Service, a nonprofit educational foundation to recruit American students to talk about democracy at international Communist youth festivals. Her mission—and that of the students—was to communicate democratic ideals throughout the world. The NSA leaders told Steinem that the program was underwritten by foundations that were funded by the Central Intelligence Agency (CIA). She thought this was a good use of government money, but many years later this prompted some people to accuse her of being a CIA agent in the women's movement. She quickly pointed out that the preposterous charge was not true. The accusations hurt her personally, nonetheless.

Steinem returned to New York in 1960. Ruth had improved after her hospital stays, and Susanne and her family were managing well. Staying in close touch with them was a top priority for Gloria, but she had to and wanted to manage on her own.

Her return to New York proved to be a smart move. Through her growing number of friends, she began to find freelance writing jobs. Gloria found encouragement to write, as well as a serious new romance with Robert Benton, art director of *Esquire* magazine. Although she later turned down his marriage proposal, they remained close professional friends. Through others at *Esquire,* Steinem met Harvey Kurtzman, one of the creators of *Mad,* who was editing a magazine of political satire called *Help! For Tired Minds.* He hired Steinem to do interviews for his cover stories, but they ended up doing the whole magazine, since there was no other staff—

Gloria shares a quiet moment with her aunt, top left, *her mother,* top right, *and her great-aunt,* seated center, *in the early 1960s.*

except for a man who did the page layout, while Harvey
supervised. That job led to more assignments from other
publications—including the *New York Times* and the
popular television series *That Was the Week That Was* a
few years later.

Still, Steinem hungered to write about the causes that
interested her: encouraging Peace Corps volunteers to
work in India; publicizing labor union organizer Cesar
Chavez's struggle for the rights of migrant farmworkers;
peacefully protesting the Vietnam War; and supporting
the Civil Rights movement.

Steinem's profound interest in the struggles of the Indian people—and in hunger and poverty throughout the
world—was not shared by many of her friends at that
time. Gradually, even Steinem's close ties to India began
to loosen, and the lessons she learned there seemed to
have no connection to her work in New York. "It wasn't
that I disliked what I was doing," she wrote. "I loved
writing satire for an *Esquire* campus issue or *That Was
the Week That Was* on television, and I enjoyed learning
about people while interviewing them—from James Bald-
win and John Lennon to Dorothy Parker and Truman
Capote. But I never felt fully engaged, as if I were leading
other than a derived life."

Steinem's contrasting qualities—her deep concern
about world problems and her attraction to show business and people in the public eye—made some people
wonder who the "real" Gloria was. But close friends who
knew her background, including her father's love of show

business and her mother's love of books, were not surprised at Steinem's easy move into many areas of New
York society. She conversed as easily with people in politics as in the arts.

Turning Points

Still uncommitted to any one social or political movement, Steinem enjoyed the freedom to explore a variety
of concerns. As writing assignments—and her income—
increased, she was able to move from her friends' apartments to one of her own. Although the new studio
apartment had only one large room, it provided more
than enough space for Steinem and her roommate, a ris-
ing artist named Barbara Nessim. Having been raised
with only the barest essentials, Steinem had long since
learned how to live without many material possessions.
As long as she had a place for her books and her typewriter and Barbara had space for her easel and paints, the
young women could comfortably focus on their careers.

Steinem's positive attitude, combined with the excitement of living among some of the country's most illustri-
ous people, propelled her in her work. New friends and
contacts multiplied, and she sometimes found herself at
parties with the very people about whom she had written.

But sad events also occurred in the 1960s. On
April 20, 1961, Steinem received the shocking news that
her father had died in a car accident in California.
Although she had had only periodic contact with him
since her parents' divorce, she still had vivid memories

Steinem in her New York apartment. Although she attended some glittery parties, most of her life consisted of long hours of work to meet story deadlines.

of him and the lessons he had taught her. He had instilled in her the value of the freedom and independence she was enjoying. The way he had treated Gloria and the way he had respected her ideas and opinions when she was just a little girl had become even more important to her as she grew older. "I loved him," she wrote, "for his sense of adventure, for looking after me when I was very little and my mother could not, and for so much more."

Perhaps her father's sense of adventure influenced Gloria's decision to accept her most unusual assignment. Although she hoped looks would not play a part in her writing career, she realized that being young and pretty would give her the opportunity to expose how young and pretty women were exploited as waitresses in the Playboy Clubs. When Steinem became a Playboy Bunny for a few weeks in 1963, even her best friends were astonished. (Bunnies were young women who waited mostly on male customers at Hugh Hefner's Playboy Clubs.)

Steinem accepted the assignment to infiltrate New York's Playboy Club on the spur of the moment, during a *Show* magazine editorial meeting. Using her grandmother's name, Marie Ochs, and stating her age as younger than her 29 years, she interviewed for the job. To her surprise, she got it. During her brief career as a Bunny, Steinem kept a day-by-day account of the experience. Despite aching, swollen feet from the flimsy high heels the Bunnies had to wear, they continued to carry trays of drinks to customers. In *Outrageous Acts and Everyday Rebellions,* Steinem described the routine:

> The Bunny tray technique involved carrying our small round trays balanced high on the palm of the left hand as we looked straight ahead and did the stylish, faintly wiggly Bunny walk. It seemed simple enough, but after an hour of carrying trays loaded

In 1963, Steinem took a job as a Playboy Club Bunny to research an article that exposed the way women were exploited at the clubs.

with ice cubes, full bottles of mixes, and a half-dozen drinks, my left arm began to shake and the blood seemed permanently drained from my fingers.

Steinem's purpose in writing the *Show* article was to reveal how the Playboy Bunnies were treated. Did they suffer demeaning remarks and actions by the customers? (They did.) Were their salaries much lower than promised? (They were.) Were their working conditions as

Publisher Clay Felker identified Steinem as a talented journalist and gave her challenging reporting assignments.

safe and healthy as advertised? (They were not.) The story published in the 1963 May and June issues of *Show* magazine brought Steinem instant fame, lawsuits, threatening phone calls—and a new identity that took years to change. She even suffered a temporary loss of "serious" writing assignments.

Nonetheless, she continued freelancing. Steinem's friend and colleague Clay Felker left his job at *Esquire* to found *New York* magazine. Steinem was among the group of writers on whose talent and intelligence Felker relied to help him develop the new periodical. She became a

As a reporter for New York *magazine, Steinem covered the riots in Harlem after the assassination of Martin Luther King in 1968.*

contributing editor and political columnist as well as a fund-raiser. "He identified her," Carolyn Heilbrun wrote, "beyond her brains and beauty, as a smart woman with whom he could work." After Martin Luther King Jr. was killed in 1968, riots broke out in cities across the country. Felker asked Steinem to go to Harlem, a mainly black section of New York City, to report on the anger that was exploding there. "Get the hell up to Harlem, and just talk to people," he said to her.

Steinem's insightful reporting caught the attention of civic and national leaders. Other assignments from *New York* included a Latin American tour with Nelson Rockefeller, then governor of New York; interviews with John Lindsay, then mayor of New York; hospital interviews with veterans from the Vietnam War; and investigations of child-care issues, antiwar protests, and the peace movement. "For the first time, I wasn't writing about one thing while caring about something else," she wrote.

Campaigns and Causes

Steinem's writing for *New York,* including "The City Politic," a column about civic issues, also recorded her campaigning for Eugene McCarthy in the 1968 presidential race. McCarthy, who had dared to challenge the war policies of Lyndon Johnson, a sitting president of his own party, became a hero in the peace movement in America. If elected, McCarthy promised to end the Vietnam War.

Steinem agreed to cover Eugene McCarthy on the campaign trail. Unlike many journalists, Steinem was able to capture the candidate in unguarded moments and zero in on details about him that revealed the man in a whole different, more human light. She wrote:

> Sitting across from the senator, I look at McCarthy slouched in his seat like a countrified Ray Milland [a movie actor during the 1940s and 1950s], and a lot of resentment falls away. I understand now why critics are crueler to directors and playwrights than to actors: it's impossible to be too tough on someone whose vulnerable human form is right before your eyes. Peering through heavy-framed reading glasses at two *New York Times* ads for Rockefeller and Humphrey, his old-fashioned suspenders stretched

Eugene McCarthy, who campaigned for the Democratic presidential nomination in 1968. Steinem covered his campaign.

over starched shirt and bony shoulders, he looks like someone's loved and overworked father poring over the family bills. A little out of place, a little re-moved—the sort of man who reads newspapers at the beach and wears street shoes with his bathing suit.

From her days as a volunteer in Adlai Stevenson's presidential campaign, Steinem had noted the concerns of women who volunteered to work in political cam-paigns. "Like other women," she wrote,

> I had either stayed at the edges doing menial jobs or been hidden away in some backroom because (a) it might be counterproductive to admit that a female was working on speeches or policy decisions, and (b) if she was under 60 and didn't have terminal acne, someone might think she was having an affair with the candidate.

The following year, in 1969, Steinem worked on a "campaign of ideas" led by Norman Mailer and Jimmy Breslin. Their candidacy for mayor and city council pres-ident of New York was serious about everything, she said, except getting elected. Eventually, Steinem dropped out of the campaign to focus her attention on the plight of the migrant farmworkers in California. Under the leader-ship of Cesar Chavez, the farmworkers were working to im-prove the terrible conditions in which they lived and worked. Chavez, a follower of Gandhi, believed in using peaceful means to protest injustice.

Cesar Chavez, front right, *used peaceful means to protest injustice, as Gandhi had. Chavez fought for better living and working conditions for farmworkers.*

With each article, Steinem's popularity grew. As her popularity increased, she herself became a cause worth fighting for—by some of New York's most talented men. She dated, among others, Tom Guinzberg, then Viking Press publisher; director Mike Nichols; and President John Kennedy's close friend and speech writer, Ted Sorensen. Her circle of friends included Broadway

Composer and musical director of the New York Philharmonic Orchestra Leonard Bernstein with his wife, Felicia

musical creators Stephen Sondheim and Jerome Robbins, as well as New York Philharmonic Orchestra conductor Leonard Bernstein and his wife, Felicia.

Steinem's friends were unanimous in hoping she would marry Mike Nichols—a very dear friend to them all. According to Carolyn Heilbrun, "Steinem felt that Felicia [Bernstein] wanted her to make the compromise Felicia had made—to give up her own identity to marry a famous man and become part of his world." But true to her nature, Steinem refused all marriage proposals, still preferring to be a free spirit and still hoping to find the work that would best blend with her convictions and the causes she supported.

The Belated Feminist

In 1969 Steinem accepted an assignment from *New York* magazine to cover a women's meeting organized by a radical feminist group called the Redstockings. That meeting, held at the Washington Square Methodist Church, turned out to be an eye-opener. In fact, it opened the door to Steinem's lifework.

At that time, abortion was illegal in the United States, but the New York legislature had recently held hearings to consider relaxing its state abortion laws. However, the legislature had invited 14 men and 1 woman—a nun—to testify. Many women were shocked and angered by the unfair composition of the people selected to testify at hearings considering abortion laws.

The meeting that proved so pivotal for Steinem was an "alternate" hearing, organized to protest the official hearings. When the Redstockings gathered at the church and began to speak, Steinem listened, not just as a journalist covering a story, but as a deeply moved woman who shared the same experience. She wrote:

> Suddenly, I was no longer learning intellectually what was wrong. I knew. I had sought and endured an abortion when I was newly out of college, but told no one. If one in three or four adult women shared this experience, why [was] each of us made to feel criminal and alone? How much power could we ever have if we had no power over the fate of our own bodies?

After attending a landmark meeting in 1969, Steinem wrote her first feminist article for New York *magazine.*

For the first time since her own 1956 abortion in London, Steinem began to question why women kept this shared experience a secret. The warmth and compassion from the women at the meeting empowered her. She never forgot the courage they showed in openly discussing the then taboo topic of abortion. That meeting was "the belated time at which feminism began to dawn on me," she later told columnist Don George. As she watched the women, one by one, rise to talk about their abortions—and the terrible consequences—Steinem used her writing ability to awaken her readers:

> I sat in a church basement listening to women stand before an audience and talk about enduring pre-abortion rapes from doctors, being asked to accept sterilization as the price of an abortion, and endangering their lives in an illegal, unsafe medical underground. It was like the "testifying" I had heard in civil rights meetings of the early sixties: emotional, rock-bottom, personal truth-telling.

After that 1969 landmark meeting, Steinem wasted no time in writing her first feminist article, "After Black Power, Women's Liberation," for *New York* magazine. In it she predicted a powerful mass movement in America, organized by women but joined by both women and men. Her story won the prestigious Penney-Missouri Award for Journalism "as one of the first aboveground reports" on the new wave of feminism in the United States.

In writing her article, Steinem tried to adhere to a standard rule of journalism—letting the facts, not her own opinions, describe the situation. But her prediction of a mass women's movement worried most of the men she knew and worked with. "Several took me aside," she recalled, "to ask kindly: Why was I writing about these crazy women instead of something serious, political, and important? How could I risk identifying myself with 'women's stuff' when I'd worked so hard to get 'real' assignments?"

In 1963, Betty Friedan wrote The Feminist Mystique. *Many people view her as the founder of the modern feminist movement.*

CHAPTER THREE

THE SECOND WAVE

This is not a bedroom war. This is a political movement.

—Betty Friedan

IN 1963 BETTY FRIEDAN'S FAMOUS, GROUND-breaking book *The Feminine Mystique* was published. (French writer Simone de Beauvoir had already made waves in Europe with her book *The Second Sex,* published in 1949.) Friedan's book focused on the plight of educated, middle-class homemakers, many of whom felt trapped, without rewarding work or a sense of self-worth. Many people view Friedan as the founder of the modern feminist movement because her book changed the lives of so many women. In urging women to rise up, leave their household chores behind them, and seek equal status with men in the workplace, Friedan struck a chord that hadn't been sounded since the suffragists called for the right to vote. In 1966, when she cofounded the National Organization for Women (NOW), choruses of women calling for equality joined in the familiar battle cry of the time, "NOW!"

Although Steinem welcomed Friedan's wake-up call to women, she felt that its focus on white, middle-class housewives did not reflect her own experience and that of other women who had always been in the paid labor force. In her article, "Life Between the Lines," Steinem explained her views:

> Despite the many early reformist virtues of *The Feminine Mystique,* it had managed to appear at the height of the civil rights movement with almost no reference to black women or other women of color. It was most relevant to the problems of the white, well-educated suburban homemakers who were standing by their kitchen sinks, wondering justifiably if there weren't "more to life than this." As a result, *white-middle-class-movement* had become the catch phrase of journalists describing feminism in the United States.

To communicate her all-inclusive message about feminism, Steinem had to do what seemed impossible. She had to conquer her lifelong fear of public speaking—because her editors were not enthusiastic about publishing more than one or two feminist articles. Her urgent need to communicate to women of all colors and cultures catapulted her into meeting rooms around the country. "I was terrified of speaking in public," she told Don George, "but

Betty Friedan cofounded the National Organization for Women in 1966. Here, she is addressing the organization's fourth annual convention in Chicago.

it mattered to me so much, this new discovery [how, together, women could change the worldview] that I ended up going out to speak."

She had been warned by friends and foes alike that "they'll stone you to death in Wichita, Kansas." Scared

but deeply committed, she went to Wichita and spoke in
a stadium that seemed full of empty seats. "I was so busy
being worried about what I was saying," she told George,
"that I didn't realize until after I left that there were
something like 8,000 people there!"

*Steinem with Dorothy Pittman Hughes, a pioneer in the creation of
child-care centers*

Writer Margaret Sloan on a speaking tour with Steinem

For support, Steinem usually teamed up with a friend and partner on the speaking tours. Her speaking partners included Dorothy Pittman Hughes, a child-care center pioneer in New York; Florynce Kennedy, a lawyer and black militant; and Margaret Sloan, a writer. The combination of Steinem and one of these three African American women attracted even broader audiences than

Steinem and writer and black militant Florynce Kennedy attracted broad audiences when on tour with their message of inclusiveness.

expected, and seeing two women together enhanced their shared message of inclusiveness. Audiences included people from all levels of society and from the peace and civil rights movements as well. African Americans understood discrimination. They had long experienced an even deeper type of second-class citizenship that feminists of all races were challenging. African American women experienced double discrimination. "I've suffered more as a woman than as a black," Shirley Chisholm, former congresswoman from New York, once said.

While on the road, Steinem came face-to-face with the opposition to feminism, but she also found that racism hadn't changed much over the years. Certain scenes remained indelible in her mind: "White train conductors in the North who let me pass into the Parlor Car, then explained to Dorothy that the cheaper seats were in the rear; Margaret standing bravely with her arms crossed to block a man storming the stage against our 'blasphemous' tale of equality; watching notorious serial killer Richard Speck explain on television that not all the women he murdered were 'like Gloria Steinem.' Although he was being interviewed in prison, his woman hatred [was] far from unique."

Frightening as the opposition became, Steinem recalls humorous moments on the tours as well. In response to Flo's 1971 book *Abortion Rap,* for example, an elderly woman cabdriver told her, "Honey, if men could get pregnant, abortion would be a sacrament." And when an angry man asked if Steinem and her friends were lesbians (as frequently happened on tour), "Flo would just look him in the eye and ask, 'Are you my alternative?'"

"It was a time," Steinem wrote, "when even one feminist speaker was a novelty, and interracial teams of feminists seemed to be unheard of since the days of

Sojourner Truth, a nineteenth-century evangelist and reformer, was a leader in the Underground Railway movement.

[abolitionist-feminist] Sojourner Truth." But Steinem's presence at rallies continued to attract huge audiences. "Her looks didn't hurt," Carolyn Heilbrun wrote. "When she had become a spokeswoman for feminism, the reassurance her appearance offered to women that . . . not all feminists resembled male truck drivers in boots and fatigues was profound."

The more Steinem spoke in public, the more confidence she gained. The more she spoke in small groups—eye-to-eye, as she had learned in India—the more she realized the special needs of women and their desire to express those needs. Since there was so much need for information on the part of women who didn't have the time or resources to

With Steinem, Brenda Feigen cofounded the Women's Action Alliance,
which worked with women at a grassroots level.

join groups or go to meetings, Steinem and lawyer Brenda
Feigen organized the Women's Action Alliance. The Alliance answered queries from women at a grassroots level
and, through the use of educational materials and programs, provided support for some of the everyday problems
women faced.

With Betty Friedan and Congresswomen Bella Abzug,
Patsy Mink, and Shirley Chisholm, Steinem founded
the National Women's Political Caucus (NWPC) in 1971.
The purpose of the caucus (a group of people united to

From left to right, *Gloria Steinem, Congresswomen Bella Abzug and Shirley Chisholm, and Betty Friedan held a press conference to announce their goal that half the delegates at presidential conventions be women.*

promote a particular cause or causes) was to unite on important issues of equality and to encourage women of all races to run for political office. At the time, a female face was not easy to find in the U.S. Congress. Some women, Steinem believed, would be motivated to succeed in government where men had failed—particularly in developing a national system of health care and child care. (The United States is the only industrial democracy without such a system.)

Steinem's popularity among women skyrocketed. Soon she became one of the most visible symbols of the

Once Steinem overcame her fear of public speaking, she became one of the most visible symbols of the feminist movement.

feminist movement in America. Yet some women accused her of "using men" to get ahead. Such criticism
was nothing new to Steinem. That type of criticism pro-
voked a central question: Because women ("the weaker
sex") had rarely achieved the same success in life that
men enjoyed, how could women possibly succeed
without strong men behind them?

Also in 1971, the president of Smith College invited
Steinem to deliver the commencement speech. Although
she felt honored, she hadn't anticipated the response her
speech, titled "The Politics of Women," would receive.
Her candid approach to society's problems—mainly
women's problems—didn't go over well with some of the
audience, especially when she called illegal abortion "the
number one health problem among women." She also
called women's housework "the only work that is noticed
if you don't do it."

An enraged Smith benefactor in the audience ex-
pressed her feelings in a letter of complaint to the college:
"That Smith College would take advantage of a captive
audience and force them to listen to such filthy dri-
vel . . . sandwiched between the Lord's Prayer and the
Benediction . . . was astounding to me, to put it mildly."

Although many of the parents were not enthusiastic,
the students gave her a standing ovation. To reach students was one thing. To reach their older, conservative
relatives was another. Steinem herself regretted the fact
that she had not realized how the words she was accustomed to using in more casual speeches might seem at a

formal commencement occasion. (A few years later, in 1978, Steinem spoke at her sister's graduation from law school in Washington and received cheers from the audience. In 1995 she was, again, the commencement speaker at Smith.)

Overturning a history of traditional thought patterns about women would not be easy. Steinem knew, for example, that the suffragists had been called "antifamily,

As many women became more empowered, signs of hostility toward the feminist movement increased.

*Pat Carbine, left, and Gloria Steinem cofounded Ms., the first maga-
zine in U.S. history to be solely owned and run by women since Susan
B. Anthony's* The Revolution.

anti-God, masculine, and unnatural women." They were sent to jail for simply pursuing the right to vote! The question was: Would history repeat itself?

Ms. America

While Steinem empowered women through her calm, caring approach to their problems, women empowered *her* to pursue their equal rights nonstop. But she missed writing about feminism and felt anxious to get back to her typewriter—despite the media's reluctance to print feminist messages. Parts of the media were actually hostile. For example, a secret memo "smuggled" out of the office of *Playboy* magazine publisher Hugh Hefner stated his opinion of feminists: "These chicks are our natural enemies....It is time to do battle with them....What I want is a devastating piece...a really expert, personal demolition job on the subject."

To combat such powerful forces, Steinem and some of her colleagues decided to publish their own magazine— one that would be owned and run solely by women—the first of its kind. But how could they get a new magazine started? Who would fund it? Who would advertise in it? Who would dare to?

"Trying to start a magazine controlled editorially and financially by its female staff in a world accustomed to the authority of men and investors should be the subject of a musical comedy," Steinem wrote. "Nonetheless, *Ms.* magazine was born." The magazine idea appealed so much to Pat Carbine, then vice president and editor in chief of *McCall's,* a traditional women's magazine, that she quit her prestigious job to cofound *Ms.* with Steinem. They chose the title *Ms.* because the early English abbreviation of the term "Mistress" included married and unmarried women—regardless of their marital status—just as "Mr." includes both single and married men.

Because Steinem had helped to start *New York* magazine a few years earlier, she relied on her many friends there for advice. She relied especially on Clay Felker. He helped Steinem jump-start *Ms.* by including 30 pages of the first issue as a supplement in the December 1971 copy of *New York.* The *Ms.* staff then launched its preview issue in January 1972. It sold out across the nation. Steinem and Carbine then went out to look for investors, and the first regular issue was published in July.

From the beginning, however, advertisers were the main problem. For one thing, only some ads promoted respect for both women and men. At a time when "carmakers were still draping blondes in evening gowns over the hoods like ornaments that could be bought with the car," the hunt for appropriate advertising was a challenge. In business meetings, men were startled to discover that Steinem wasn't "shrill" and "man-hating" as the feminists had been portrayed by much of the media. In fact they were charmed by her personality and impressed by her success.

No one enjoyed Steinem's success more than her mother. "She was very proud of my being a published writer," Steinem wrote. "She was also overly appreciative

Steinem at the Ms. office in 1972. Even the founders were pleasantly surprised by the popularity of the magazine.

of any presents given to her, and that made giving them irresistible. I loved to send her clothes, exotic soaps, and additions to her collection of tarot cards."

In spite of her busy schedule, Gloria frequently visited Ruth and Susanne and her family. Gloria also arranged to have her mother visit her in New York. The bond between them remained close, but Steinem's increasing fame invited the media's curiosity about her family.

Despite Steinem's busy schedule, she and her mother, shown here in 1970, remained close.

Knowing that memories of the Toledo days depressed Ruth, Steinem pleaded with reporters not to invade her mother's privacy. Nevertheless, they did so. "They published things that hurt her very much and sent her into a downhill slide," Steinem wrote. But such events never stopped Ruth from going out in public. "She was quite capable," Steinem wrote, "of putting a made-up name on her name tag when going to her conventional women's club where she feared our shared identity would bring controversy or even just questions."

Gloria, on the other hand, was enjoying her new sense of community with all the women working at *Ms.* magazine. As *Ms.* blossomed in the national limelight, however, so did its critics. A fringe of the women's movement thought the magazine was too lenient toward men and that equal rights could never be gained in a capitalist society. But readers from pioneering feminist organizations such as the National Organization for Women encouraged *Ms.* in its promotion of the Equal Rights Amendment (ERA), reproductive freedom, exposing violence against women, and other important issues. Steinem welcomed *all* readers' views; she liked the dialogue. "We never would have continued if readers hadn't encouraged us," she wrote. Summing up the importance of *Ms.,* former employee Harriet Lyons wrote, "This was the magazine that first exposed the extent of the problem of battered wives, sexual harassment—we broke it first."

Woman of the Year

In 1972, following the successful launching of *Ms.* magazine, Steinem and her colleagues started the Ms. Foundation for Women. They wanted to establish the Ms. Foundation because at that time, few, if any, foundations gave money to women's causes. Independent from the magazine, the foundation began to promote empowerment and self-esteem in women of all races through programs that both educate and give grants to grassroots

At a news conference, Steinem announces that through the Ms. Foundation, $2 million in loans have been given to help low-income women get started in business. Forescee Hogan, right, works with the program in Los Angeles.

activists. One of its best-known endeavors has been the Take Our Daughters to Work Day—a unique project that informs and inspires young women around the world. Steinem explained in an interview:

> Take Our Daughters to Work Day . . . is the only day each year when the spotlight is on girls' hopes, dreams, and talents. Parents and friends of girls are encouraged to invite girls into the workplace. Future employers create programs for classes of girls. And the boys who remain in school have a special curriculum on gender that will enable them to be more equal friends, co-workers, and parents in the future. Now a nationwide and international day of recognition, Take Our Daughters to Work Day lets young girls know they are visible, valuable, and heard.

During a Take Our Daughters to Work Day, one young woman visits her father's construction site, while another examines a water main with her mother.

In addition to overseeing many projects and writing articles (more than 150 by 1972), Steinem became active in the 1972 presidential campaign of George McGovern, a Democratic senator from South Dakota. She came to the campaign armed with a feminist agenda that included the important issue of reproductive freedom—the right to decide when and whether to have children—which includes contraception and abortion as well as safe childbirth and freedom from coerced sterilization.

Steinem became active in the 1972 presidential campaign of George McGovern, a Democratic senator from South Dakota.

Congresswoman Shirley Chisholm addresses the 1972 Democratic National Convention in Miami, Florida.

Steinem and other feminists hoped to incorporate this principle into the Democratic Party's platform, the statement of issues a political party considers most important. In addition, however, she ran as a delegate pledged to Shirley Chisholm. Chisholm, who was also campaigning for the Democratic presidential nomination, was the first black woman to serve in the U.S. Congress. Although she did not have enough support to win the presidential nomination, Steinem said, "She could and did use her candidacy to educate people about the issues and to take the 'white males only' sign off the White House in the national imagination."

In Miami, where the Democratic National Convention was held, the National Women's Political Caucus formed a powerful voice for feminist goals and won most of them. Although reproductive freedom was not included in the platform, other issues were. The presence of so many strong women participating in the decision-making process encouraged many more to participate in the future. As the elected Democratic spokesperson for the National Women's Political Caucus, Steinem was pleased that most NWPC goals—especially the assurance of more women members of state delegations—were realized.

But Steinem's increasing prominence as the chief spokesperson—a role she did not seek—alienated some of the movement's pioneers, such as Betty Friedan. Until Steinem joined the feminist movement, many people had considered Friedan to be its leader, and Friedan was not used to being overshadowed. Also, the Redstockings, who had originally hailed Steinem's participation, turned against her. They claimed that their group had been eclipsed by Steinem and everything she touched—including *Ms.* The magazine, they said, wasn't radical enough. And there were, indeed, differences of opinion among the various factions of the women's movement. Some women's groups disagreed with each other on issues such as abortion, lesbian rights, and welfare rights.

In the midst of the social and political debate, Steinem had become a star—even though she refused to be photographed or to cooperate with some of the articles being written. When members of the media latched onto her,

Gloria Steinem, speaking here at the 1972 Democratic National Convention, was named Woman of the Year by McCall's *magazine.*

there was no stopping them. Pictures and stories about her appeared in *Newsweek, Time, People,* and countless newspapers around the world. *McCall's* named Steinem Woman of the Year in 1972. That same year, the prestigious National Press Club in Washington, D.C., selected her as the first woman in its history to speak there. Indeed, her demand to be taken seriously had been met.

Steinem was the first woman in history to speak at the prestigious National Press Club in Washington, D.C.

Few women, it seemed, could deliver the feminist message more effectively than Gloria Steinem.

In 1974 Steinem met Stan Pottinger. Deciding not to marry didn't mean she wanted to be without male friends and lovers, however, and she began a nine-year relationship with him. Pottinger worked in the administrations of both Republican president Richard Nixon and Democratic president Jimmy Carter as head of the civil rights division of the Justice Department. Besides Ohio roots, Steinem and Pottinger shared a dedication to the same goal—equal rights and equal opportunities for all Americans regardless of their sex, race, ethnic origin, religion, or sexual orientation. He was a strong supporter of equal rights for women in every area from employment to credit. He helped Steinem in her efforts to win support and to strategize legal tactics.

Two major developments heightened awareness of women's issues around the world. When the United

Coretta Scott King, left, *wife of deceased civil rights leader Martin Luther King Jr., asked the National Women's Conference to draft a resolution on minorities and their problems. Steinem is on the right. The woman in the middle is unidentified.*

Congresswoman Bella Abzug of New York, left, headed the 1977 International Women's Year commission in Houston, Texas. Tennis star Billie Jean King addressed the audience.

Nations proclaimed 1975 as International Women's Year, it sparked discussions from New York to New Delhi. Topics of discussion included equal rights, human rights, malnutrition, poverty, contraception, abortion, and other issues. In 1977 President Jimmy Carter followed up with an International Women's Year commission to bring together women from every state for a national conference that had been proposed by Bella Abzug and other women in Congress. He appointed Steinem among the 40 commissioners who would organize the project—another first of its kind—to be held in Houston, Texas. The commission was headed by Congresswoman Bella Abzug.

Women representing every race, color, religion, and culture in the country went to the Houston conference in November 1977. They voted for a historic measure to prohibit discrimination based on sexual orientation. "Houston was the first public landmark in a long, suspicion-filled journey across racial barriers," Steinem wrote. "At last, there were enough women of color (more than one-third of all the delegates) . . . to have a strong voice." There were also more women from different Native American tribes and nations meeting together nationally than ever before. In "Houston and History," Steinem called the conference a landmark in her personal history, and revealed the anxiety that had plagued her prior to the event:

> I had learned, finally, that *individual women* could be competent, courageous, and loyal to each other. . . .

Stan Pottinger shared Steinem's dedication to equal rights and equal opportunities for all people.

But I still wasn't sure that *women as a group* could be competent, courageous, and loyal to each other. I didn't believe that we could conduct large, complex events, in all our diversity, and make history on our own. But we can. Houston taught us that.

In 1977, Steinem won the Woodrow Wilson Scholarship from the Smithsonian Institution in Washington to pursue her study of feminism in America. The scholarship meant that she would have a year at the Woodrow

Wilson Center in Washington, D.C., to do research in the Library of Congress and to write. She wanted to write a book on the impact of feminism on political theory, but the many other demands on her time prevented her from completing the project. She researched and wrote several essays instead. Living in Washington for a year also meant that she could spend more time with Pottinger and his three children, as well as with her own family. Steinem needed all the support she could get at that time, because the last major struggle to enact the Equal Rights Amendment (ERA) was about to begin.

Alice Paul first brought the Equal Rights Amendment before the U.S. Congress in 1923.

∎

A TIME TO
MARCH

They are awake and moving toward their
goal like a tidal wave.

—Martin Luther King Jr.

IN *MS.* MAGAZINE, STEINEM WROTE ABOUT CAUSES
closest to her heart, but she also raised the consciousness
of others at the same time. Her "on the road" discussions
of women's rights became invaluable as she traveled on
behalf of the Equal Rights Amendment, which Congress
passed in 1972. Ratification (or approval) by three-fourths
of the state legislatures is required for any amendment to
be added to the U.S. Constitution.

The Equal Rights Amendment states: "Equality of
rights under the law shall not be denied or abridged by
the United States or by any state on account of sex." Over
the next several years, feminists fanned out in hundreds

Phyllis Schlafly of the conservative Eagle Forum, standing center with hands in pockets, *was one of the leading opponents of the Equal Rights Amendment.*

of campaigns across the country to encourage adoption of the ERA. More than 30 states ratified the amendment within one year. But in the remaining states, women faced tough opposition from some members of the Republican Party and various right-wing groups who did everything in their power to prevent the ERA's ratification. One of the ERA's most vocal opponents was Phyllis Schlafly of the right-wing Eagle Forum. She and her many followers—including members of conservative religious groups—claimed that the ERA was "pro-abortion, pro-gay rights," and that it supported many other issues that never appeared in the amendment.

Opponents also claimed that the amendment would result in women being forced to work outside the home;

On July 9, 1978, more than 100,000 people marched to the Capitol in Washington, D.C., in support of the Equal Rights Amendment. From left to right, *leaders of the march included Congresswoman Bella Abzug, Gloria Steinem, comedian Dick Gregory, Betty Friedan, and Congresswomen Barbara Mikulski and Margaret Heckler. The woman to the right is unidentified.*

women having to fight and die in war; women having to lose all alimony in a divorce; and other misconceptions. Steinem responded to a *New York Times* report about the greatly misunderstood amendment, saying:

> The ERA has nothing to do with whether gays adopt children, does not increase the power of the Federal government, does not lead to unisex toilets; it increases the rights of women who work at home. . . . No one in their right mind is pro-abortion. . . . The accurate phrase is pro-choice.

Steinem went into high gear in support of the ERA, appearing on television and radio, in village greens, and—most effectively and most often—in print. To express the diversity and depth of women's concerns, in addition to the ERA, *Ms.* magazine put together a production team headed by Joan Shigekawa to create *Women Alive,* a PBS series that featured women's issues and profiles of important women activists and artists.

But the seven-year deadline for ratification was approaching. It took a major show of support—100,000 people marching in Washington, D.C.—to win an extension to the ERA ratification deadline. The National Organization for Women organized the event, the largest march on

At a 1978 House Judiciary Committee meeting, Gloria Steinem, left, and presidential assistant Midge Costanza learn that the ERA will get an extension for ratification.

behalf of women's rights in history. Steinem and countless other dedicated feminists around the country gave
their time and energy to the event. The march took place
on July 9, 1978—the anniversary of the death of suffragist
Alice Paul, who had first brought the Equal Rights
Amendment before Congress in 1923. The amendment
won an extension—to June 30, 1982—and the battle for
ratification by the remaining states continued. Positive
support from the march invigorated and united women.

Although Steinem was happy about the progress being
made by the women's movement, an event in her personal life caused her great unhappiness. By 1981, Ruth
Steinem's health had worsened. She needed full-time
nursing, so she moved to a nursing home near Susanne's
house. "If I ever had any doubts about the debt we owe to
nurses," Steinem wrote, "those last months laid them to
rest." Both Gloria and Susanne took turns staying by
their mother's side when Ruth approached death, following a stroke in July 1981. "I realize now," Gloria wrote,
"why I've always been more touched by old people than
by children. It's the talent and hopes locked up in a fail-
ing body and unsure mind that get to me—a poignant
contrast that reminds me of my mother, even when
she was strong."

Gloria and Susanne had no difficulty selecting the
church for Ruth's memorial service. "Her memorial service was in the Episcopalian church that she loved because it fed the poor, let the homeless sleep in its pews,
had members of almost every race, and had been sued by

the Episcopalian hierarchy for having a woman priest."
Steinem noted that her mother had given some of her
Michigan property to this church "in the hope that it
could be used as a multiracial camp, thus getting even
with those neighbors who had snubbed my father for
being Jewish."

Steinem found it difficult to express her personal feelings in writing, but when she did, the results, critics said,
were "unforgettable." Here is an example taken from the
closing passage of "Ruth's Song":

> I miss her—but perhaps no more in death than I did
> in life. Dying seems less sad than having lived too lit-
> tle. But at least we're now asking questions about all
> the Ruths in all our family mysteries. If her song in-
> spires that, I think she would be the first to say: It
> was worth the singing.

Coming Together

"I'm only going to do this for two years," Steinem once
said, as the overwhelming task of creating the first feminist magazine began. Ten years later, in 1982, she found
herself center stage at the 10th anniversary celebration of
Ms. magazine. And there was real cause to celebrate. De-
scribing the early problems of *Ms.,* Steinem told Don
George, "We were running it with mirrors and Scotch
tape, and it's a miracle that it managed to survive."

Although the ERA had not been ratified and the ratification deadline was just a few weeks away, Steinem

In January 1985, Gloria Steinem, left, honored Geraldine Ferraro, center—the first woman to run for vice president on a major party ticket—and popular rock star Cyndi Lauper, right, as Ms. magazine's Women of the Year.

could point to countless ways in which feminism had changed women's lives in America. In the 10th anniversary issue of *Ms.*, she listed some of them:

- **Now,** we are becoming the men we wanted to marry. Ten years ago, we were trained to marry a doctor, not be one.
- **Now,** we have words like "sexual harassment" and "battered women." Ten years ago, it was just called "life."
- **Now,** there is 70 percent national agreement on the reality and wrongness of sex discrimination. Ten

Astronaut Shannon Lucid spent a record 188 days in space aboard the Russian Mir *space station in 1996.* Newsweek *magazine said, "It was one large step for a woman, one small step for NASA's new breed of astronaut."*

years ago, the majority thought there was no discrimination, and women were still being punished
for an illusion of power; white women "controlled
the economy" and black women were "matriarchs."

• **Now,** there are women astronauts. Ten years ago,
NASA's idea of women was "sexual diversion" on
"long-duration flights such as Mars."

• **Now,** women police officers are accepted—and
popular heroes on TV series like "Hill Street Blues"
and "Cagney and Lacey." Ten years ago, policemen
protested—and organized their wives to demon-
strate—against the very idea of policewomen.

• **Now,** networks of women-helping-women are a
force in every town, profession, racial and eco-
nomic group. Ten years ago, mostly white groups of
women were still consciousness-raising in the privacy of living rooms.

- **Now,** the first woman in history is a Justice of the U.S. Supreme Court. Ten years ago, the only woman was the blindfolded statue.
- **Now,** 359 national companies offer maternity leave, and 34 offer paternity leave. Ten years ago, the first was a privilege—and the second wasn't even a term.

In 1984 another gala celebration took place. More than 700 people gathered at the Waldorf Astoria in New York to celebrate Steinem's 50th birthday and raise funds for the Ms. Foundation. Syndicated columnist Liz Smith called the event "a social 'love-in' on a grand scale." A wide variety of guests attended the party, including talk-

Actor Alan Alda embraces Gloria Steinem at her 50th birthday party. The gala party raised money for the Ms. Foundation.

show host Phil Donahue, actresses Marlo Thomas and
Bette Midler, civil rights pioneer Rosa Parks, and astronaut Sally Ride. The night was filled with joy and overwhelming support of the Ms. Foundation—the umbrella
over so many projects that have been crucial to the ad-
vancement of women. The creation of jobs for women
and businesses cooperatively owned by women are just
two of the foundation's many concerns that have bene-
fited from the 1984 fund-raiser.

Just two years later, in the spring of 1986, Steinem received some devastating news. During a regular physical
checkup, doctors discovered that a tiny lump that had
seemed harmless in a mammogram was actually breast
cancer. With no family history of cancer, the news
shocked Gloria. Yet she reacted in her typical show-must-
go-on fashion. A couple of months before the diagnosis,
she had agreed to appear as a substitute cohost for a week
on the popular morning television show *Today,* and she
did appear on the program before going into the hospital
for a lymph node test that followed the original biopsy.

Neither that surgery, which showed no lymph node involvement, nor radiation therapy stopped Steinem from
participating in events to help others. In 1986 and 1987,
she represented New York and northern New Jersey on
the Citizens Committee on AIDS. Approximately 15 foundations formed the committee. Carolyn Heilbrun described the impact Steinem had on the courageous
people she met there. Tom Stoddard, a lawyer and gay
activist, particularly admired her. Stoddard, who later

Steinem, standing center, *served on the Citizens Committee on AIDS, which explored nonmedical problems related to the disease and recommended solutions.*

disclosed that he had been diagnosed as HIV positive, said: "She is a peacemaker, an extraordinary combination of change-maker and peacemaker. I was stunned to find a celebrity who was genuinely humble and kind."

Through her diagnosis and accompanying therapy, Steinem learned to focus on her own health and well-being as she had focused on those of others. She began to examine her own thoughts and feelings and to see how the past had come together with the present. Her early responsibility for her mother had helped shape her lifelong commitment to help others. She also began to understand how her love of learning, rooted in her childhood, had opened so many doors for her.

Steinem, on a book promotion tour, spoke at a fund-raiser for the Metropolitan Women's Center in Columbus, Ohio. She said that "the price you pay for living a rebellious life is nothing compared to the price you pay for not rebelling."

Steinem's success as an author boomed in the 1980s. Already well known for her feminist leadership and her role as a journalist, she began to make headlines with her books. *Outrageous Acts and Everyday Rebellions,* published in 1984 (with a second edition in 1995), is a moving and informative collection of some of her early feminist pieces. A book about movie star Marilyn

Monroe, called *Marilyn: Norma Jeane,* was published in 1986. *Revolution from Within,* which deals with the link between self-esteem and social changes, followed in 1992. And *Moving beyond Words,* published in 1994, offers reflections on Steinem's past—but with an eye to the future. "I'm not sure feminism should require an adjective," she wrote. "But if I were to choose only one adjective, I still would opt for *radical* feminist. I know patriarchs keep equating the word with *violent* or *man-hating, crazy* or *extremist.* . . . Nonetheless, *radical* seems an honest indication of the fundamental change we have

From left to right, *Dr. Ruth Westheimer, Gloria Steinem, and actress Marlo Thomas pose during a press conference in Boston, Massachusetts, preceding a fund-raiser for the Ms. Foundation.*

in mind and says what probably is the case: the false division of human nature into 'feminine' and 'masculine' is the root of all other divisions into subject and object, active and passive—the beginning of hierarchy."

To promote her books—and the causes of social justice—Steinem once again traveled widely, trying to help empower women wherever she went. One of the media highlights was a television interview with Barbara Walters, cohost of ABC's *20/20*. The tap-dancing star from Toledo, Ohio, performed a song and dance routine with Walters on national TV—having said she would only say yes to Walters' request if Walters sang. To Steinem's surprise, Barbara Walters said yes. They later performed together at a Carnegie Hall benefit.

Over the years, the great success of *Ms.* influenced other women's magazines to publish more feminist articles, but advertisers continued to withhold support unless there were traditional articles on fashion, beauty, and food. Because *Ms.* wouldn't compromise its editorial content to get ads, it gradually accumulated debt and had to be sold. At the urging of two Australian women, feminist journalist Anne Summers and her publishing partner Sandra Yates, the media firm Fairfax purchased the magazine in 1987. They could not break the advertising bias either. *Ms.* was taken over by Lang Communications in 1989 and was reborn as an ad-free magazine in 1990. "We realized," Steinem said years later, "it was established enough that women would pay for it, as you do when you buy a book."

Anita Hill, left, and Gloria Steinem, right, participate in a 1992 conference on sexual harassment. Hill accused Supreme Court Justice Clarence Thomas of sexual harassment while she had worked for him.

The 1980s and early 1990s also brought some fierce opposition to the women's movement. During the Reagan and Bush administrations (1981–1993), the conservative religious right, organized as a group called the Christian Coalition, and various other groups tried to erode and overturn the 1973 *Roe v. Wade* decision that had legalized abortion in the United States. They also tried to bring an end to women's reproductive freedom by passing antiabortion restrictions—especially for young women and poor women, who had less political power—in every state possible. Many feminist groups, such as the National Organization for Women and the National Women's Political Caucus, were effective in blocking their efforts and defending the basic right to abortion, but restrictions on federal funding and the promotion of parental consent seriously eroded it.

Because the feminist movement had been so successful in increasing the number of women in the workplace and enacting laws to protect them against sexual harassment and discrimination, some men wondered if women had achieved "enough" and should "go back home." Fearful of women's equality and still feeling threatened by the growing power of women, some men spoke out. In March 1992, *Time* magazine featured "The War against Feminism" as its cover story. Interviewed for an article in that issue, Steinem said: "Once you get a majority consciousness change, you also get a backlash. It's both an inevitable tribute and a danger. The future depends entirely on what each of us does every day. After all, a movement is only people moving."

Over 60 years old and still going strong, Steinem hopes the future will bring "the personal and the political, the heart and the mind, the high-tech and the high-touch" closer together. In her 27 years of traveling around the United States, she has seen the positive results from small gatherings of women who meet regularly to support

Ardent feminists Bella Abzug, left, *and Gloria Steinem,* right, *attend a Democratic Party meeting in New York.*

each other, and she continues to foster that movement. She said in a GNN (on-line) interview:

> We need the small groups—10 or 12 who meet to-gether . . . and share the same interests. We are mak-ing alternate families, communities of interest, and we need that kind of support. . . . In the civil rights movement it was called the "rap group"; in the women's movement, it was the "consciousness-raising group" and then "networking"; and now it's often a book club. I think that's crucial, that kind of all-five-senses experience.

Steinem with President Bill Clinton at a Women's Power Lunch in New York. Clinton is shaking hands with Jewell Jackson McCabe, cochair of the event with Steinem.

In *Moving beyond Words*, Steinem warned of the danger involved in reviving "the good old days before women and men of every race were seeking equal power." "Clinging to the past is the problem," she wrote. "Embracing change is the solution." Echoes of Gandhian philosophy also continue to permeate Steinem's words and actions and to resonate in her meetings with women around the world: "I find the wisdom of our Ramnad team leader still holds true: 'You have to listen . . . you have to know . . . you have to sit down eye-to-eye.'"

At a Convocation for Peace at Women's Health Centers, Steinem speaks from the pulpit of the Cathedral of St. John the Divine in New York City.

NEW FOOTSTEPS

And so encourage one another and help one
another, just as you are doing.

—1 Thessalonians 5:11

GLORIA STEINEM HAS HAD AN IMPACT ON THE
lives of many women. She has indirectly inspired every
shelter for battered women, every family crisis center,
and countless women's organizations across America.
Many such places exist because of her activism and
undaunted leadership. But Steinem still hopes that in
helping "to overthrow the patriarchal, racist, and other
hierarchies that weaken self-esteem in some and make it
falsely dependent on domination in others," shelters and
crisis centers will one day become obsolete. In 1996,

Steinem at a girls' conference in connection with Girls Speak Out at the United Nations.

Steinem—together with Andrea Johnston, a teacher from northern California—concentrated on Girls Speak Out, a project sponsored by the Ms. Foundation. The project, she says, is like Talks for Girls—

> . . . what Virginia Woolf called her effort to get women's history out of the classroom and into the hands of young girls. It's for girls 9 to 15. We do two consecutive weekends of meetings. It's kind of old-fashioned consciousness raising for young girls. It's

Steinem, right, next to Jacqueline Kennedy Onassis at an Academy of Arts and Letters gathering in New York. The other woman is not identified.

> inside-out education, not outside-in. . . . Everything
> comes out of the girls and I've really been enjoying
> that. Girls at 9, 10, and 11 are so much themselves be-
> fore they've been hit by the feminine role, and it's
> great to listen to them and learn from them. We are
> trying to encourage them to value themselves and
> value their uniqueness.

And what does Steinem tell girls who want to follow in her footsteps?

> We are communal creatures, but I think the sense of
> ourselves as unique is what's most missing. So I
> would say just trust your instincts . . . and what you
> are drawn to, what most interests you . . . what ex-
> cites you. Do that every day and you'll end up mak-
> ing a new map, new footsteps.

Because of the paths Steinem helped to forge in the feminist movement, American women of all ages have more freedom than ever before. "We owe a lot to Gloria Steinem," Jacqueline Kennedy Onassis said. "Purpose, persistence, and style have characterized her leadership, and all of us are the better for it."

POSTSCRIPT

MANY WOMEN WORK OUTSIDE THE HOME BECAUSE they have to, but thanks to the women's movement, greater opportunities and protections—only pipe dreams in the 1950s—are now available.

More than a third of all businesses in the United States are owned by women. Typically, women earn 74 to 95 cents for every dollar men earn, up from 57 cents in 1972. But women are making nearly the same salaries as men in some jobs, such as those of computer analysts. Also, the Platform for Action that emerged from the 1995 United Nations Fourth World Conference on Women in Beijing, China, is expected to strengthen women's power in workplaces around the world—especially in poor countries.

"Finding and speaking in our own voice—and helping others to do the same—is still the key," Steinem says.

S O U R C E S

7   Gloria Steinem, "The Stage Is Set," *Ms.* (August, 1982), 77, 78, 228.

9   Gloria Steinem, *Revolution from Within* (Boston: Little, Brown, 1992), 69.

12   Carolyn Heilbrun, *The Education of a Woman* (New York: Dial Press, 1995), 16.

16   Gloria Steinem, *Outrageous Acts and Everyday Rebellions* (New York: Holt, Rinehart & Winston, Second Ed., 1995), 143.

18   Heilbrun, *The Education of a Woman,* 20.

21   Steinem, *Outrageous Acts and Everyday Rebellions,*132.

22   Heilbrun, *The Education of a Woman,* 28.

24   Steinem, *Outrageous Acts and Everyday Rebellions,*145.

25   Heilbrun, *The Education of a Woman,* 31.

30   Steinem, *Glamour,* (August, 1964), 148.

33   Steinem, *Revolution from Within,* 113.

39   Gloria Steinem, *Moving beyond Words* (New York: Simon & Schuster, 1994), 265, 266.

40   Ibid., 267.

41   Ibid., 266.

41   Heilbrun, *The Education of a Woman,* 85.

44   Steinem, *Moving beyond Words,* 268.

46   Steinem, *Revolution from Within,* 232.

47   Steinem, *Outrageous Acts and Everyday Rebellions,* 62.

51   Heilbrun, *The Education of a Woman,* 134.

51   Steinem, *Outrageous Acts and Everyday Rebellions,* 20.

52–53   Steinem, *Outrageous Acts and Everyday Rebellions,* 21,89.

55   Heilbrun, *The Education of a Woman,* 119.

56   Steinem, *Outrageous Acts and Everyday Rebellions,* 21.

58   Ibid., 22.

59   Ibid., 7.

62   Steinem, *Outrageous Acts and Everyday Rebellions,* 7.

62–64   "Gloria Steinem—On the Web," Interview with Don George (GNN, Internet) April 25, 1996.

67   Steinem, *Outrageous Acts and Everyday Rebellions,* 10, 11, 8.

68   Heilbrun, *The Education of a Woman,* 122.

72   Heilbrun, *The Education of a Woman,* 197.

73 Steinem, *Outrageous Acts and Everyday Rebellions,* 384.

75 Steinem, *Outrageous Acts and Everyday Rebellions,* 6, 7.

76–77 Ibid., 152, 153.

79 Heilbrun, *The Education of a Woman,* 257.

80 "Gloria Steinem—On the Web"

83 Correspondence with the author.

89–90 Steinem, *Outrageous Acts and Everyday Rebellions,* 315, 316.

95 Heilbrun, *The Education of a Woman,* 321.

97–98 Steinem, *Outrageous Acts and Everyday Rebellions,* 154, 155, 158.

98 "Gloria Steinem—On the Web."

99–101 Steinem, *Ms.* (August, 1982), 77–78.

103 Heilbrun, *The Education of a Woman,* 386.

105–106 Steinem, *Moving beyond Words,* 270.

106 "Gloria Steinem—On the Web."

108 Steinem quoted in *Time,* March 9, 1992, 57.

109 "Gloria Steinem—On the Web."

110–111 Steinem, *Moving beyond Words,* 274.

113 Correspondence with the author.

114–116 "Gloria Steinem—On the Web."

116 Onassis quoted in *Ms.,* (August 1982), 95.

117 Correspondence with the author.

B I B L I O G R A P H Y

Books

Davis, Flora. *Moving the Mountain: The Women's Movement in America since 1960.* New York: Simon & Schuster, 1991.

Echols, Alice. *Daring to Be Bad: Feminism in America 1967–1975.* Minneapolis: University of Minnesota Press, 1989.

Eisler, Bernita. *Private Lives: Men and Women of the Fifties.* New York: Franklin Watts, 1986.

Evans, Sara. *Personal Politics: The Roots of Women's Liberation in the Civil Rights Movement and the New Left.* New York: Vintage Books, 1980.

Faludi, Susan. *Backlash.* New York: Crown, 1991.

Friedan, Betty. *The Feminine Mystique.* New York: Norton, 1973.

_____. *It Changed My Life: Writings on the Women's Movement.* New York: Random House, 1976.

Heilbrun, Carolyn. *The Education of a Woman: The Life of Gloria Steinem.* New York: Dial Press, 1995.

Kennedy, Florynce. *Color Me Flo: My Hard Life and Good Times.* New Jersey: Prentice Hall, 1976.

Millett, Kate. *Flying.* New York: Alfred A. Knopf, 1974.

Morgan, Robin, ed. *Sisterhood Is Powerful.* New York: Vintage Books, 1970.

_____. *Sisterhood Is Global.* New York: Doubleday, 1984.

Steinem, Gloria. *Outrageous Acts and Everyday Rebellions.*
New York: Holt, Rinehart & Winston, 1983.

_____. *Marilyn: Norma Jeane.* New York: Holt, Rinehart &
Winston, 1986.

_____. *Revolution from Within.* Boston: Little, Brown Co., 1992.

_____. *Moving beyond Words.* New York: Simon & Schuster,
1994.

Walker, Alice. *In Search of Our Mothers' Gardens.* New York:
Harcourt Brace Jovanovich, 1983.

Warren, Robert Penn et al. *American Literature: The Makers
and the Making.* Vol. 11. New York: St. Martin's Press,
1973.

Articles

Attinger, Joelle. "Steinem: Tying Politics to the Personal."
Time, March 9, 1992, 55.

Barthel, Joan. "The Glorious Triumph of Gloria Steinem."
Cosmopolitan, March 1984, 217–219.

Bumiller, Elizabeth. "Gloria Steinem: Two Decades of
Feminism and the Fire Burns as Bright." *Washington Post,*
October 12, 1983.

Dullea, Georgia. "Birthday Celebration: Gloria Steinem at 50."
New York Times, May 24, 1984.

Gibbs, Nancy. "The War against Feminism." *Time,* March 9,
1992, 50–55.

_____ and Jeanne McDowell. "How to Revive a Revolution,"
Time, March 9, 1992, 56–57.

Levitt, Leonard. "She: The Awesome Power of Gloria Steinem." *Esquire,* October 17, 1971, 87.

Mercer, M. "McCall's Woman of the Year." *McCall's,* January 1972, 67–69.

Steinem, Gloria. Numerous articles. *Ms.,* 1972–1996.

On-Line Publications

George, Don. "Gloria Steinem—On the Web," Global Network Navigator (GNN), April 20, 1996.

PHOTO   ACKNOWLEDGMENTS

AP/Wide World Photos, 2-3, 46, 49, 55, 57, 70, 80, 81 (bottom), 85, 87, 88, 95, 96, 101, 103, 105, 107, 109, 110, 112; © Archive Photos, 83; Bettman, 74; Dan Borris/Outline, 3; Frank Capril/Saga/Archive Photos, 60; Corbis-Bettmann, 52, 68; © Michael Ginsburg/Magnum Photos, Inc., 71; New York Times Co./Archive Photos, 6; Minnesota Historical Society, 28; Paul Thomas, 65; National Aeronautics and Space Administration (NASA), 8 (top); Reuters/Corbis-Bettmann, 8 (bottom); © Frances M. Roberts, 81 (top); Russell Reif/Archive Photos, 73; Joe Skipper/Reuters/Archive Photos, 100; courtesy of Gloria Steinem, 10, 13, 14, 15, 17, 20, 23, 26, 31, 32, 38, 43, 64, 66 (© Ray Bald), 69 (with permission of Brenda Feigen), 77, 78, 90; UPI/Corbis-Bettmann, 35, 48, 50, 54, 63, 82, 86, 92, 94, 99, 104, 115; Jennifer Warburg, 114.

Front cover photo © Dan Borris/Outline; back cover photo © Frank Ockenfels/Outline.

ABOUT THE AUTHOR

Caroline E. Lazo has written many books for children and young adults, including a biography of Arthur Ashe for Lerner Publications. She has also written extensively about art and architecture. Ms. Lazo pursued her interest in international relations at the University of Oslo in Norway and received a B. A. in art history from the University of Minnesota.

Lerner's **Newsmakers** series:
Muhammad Ali: Champion
Ray Charles: Soul Man
The 14th Dalai Lama: Spiritual Leader of Tibet
Sir Edmund Hillary: To Everest and Beyond
Marilyn Monroe: Norma Jeane's Dream
Steven Spielberg: Master Storyteller
Gloria Steinem: Feminist Extraordinaire
Aung San Suu Kyi: Fearless Voice of Burma